THE HUMAN PATH ACROSS THE CONTINENTS

PATHWAYS THROUGH SOUTH AMERICA

Heather C. Hudak

BOISE PUBLIC LIBRARY

CRABTREE
PUBLISHING COMPANY
WWW.CRABTREEBOOKS.COM

CRABTREE
PUBLISHING COMPANY
WWW.CRABTREEBOOKS.COM

Author: Heather C. Hudak

Editorial director: Kathy Middleton

Editors: Rachel Cooke, Janine Deschenes

Design: Jeni Child

Photo research: FFP Consulting; Tammy McGarr

Proofreader: Melissa Boyce

Prepress and production coordinator: Tammy McGarr

Print coordinator: Katherine Berti

Produced for Crabtree Publishing Company by
FFP Consulting Limited

Images:
t=Top, b=Bottom, tl=Top Left, tr=Top Right, bl=Bottom Left,
br=Bottom Right, c=Center, lc=Left Center, rc=Right Center

Alamy
Jesse KraftL p. 9t; Paul Thompson Images: p. 10 bl; Nicholas
Tinelli: p. 14–15b; National Geographic Image Collection:
p. 15tl; EFE News Agency: p. 29br
iStock
EduLeite: p. 7rc; olli0815: p. 13br; Rudimencial: p. 19t; cifotart:
p. 25rc
Shutterstock
Art Konovalov: p. 7t; Gualberto Becerra: p. 9lc; elbud: p. 16bl;
NRuArg: p. 17t; Peek Creative Collective: p. 17b; Guaxinim:
p. 18l; gary yim: p. 20bl; Nowaczyk: p. 22b; Anton_Ivanov:
p. 26bl; Marcel Bakker: p. 27b; Matyas Rehak: p. 29t

All other images from Shutterstock

Maps: Jeni Child

Library and Archives Canada Cataloguing in Publication

Title: Pathways through South America / Heather C. Hudak.
Names: Hudak, Heather C., 1975- author.
Description: Series statement: The human path across the continents |
  Includes index.
Identifiers: Canadiana (print) 20190112123 | Canadiana (ebook) 20190112131
  ISBN 9780778766438 (hardcover)
  ISBN 9780778766506 (softcover)
  ISBN 9781427124029 (HTML)
Subjects: LCSH: Human ecology—South America—Juvenile literature. |
  LCSH: South America—Juvenile literature.
Classification: LCC GF531 .H83 2019 | DDC j304.2098—dc23

Library of Congress Cataloging-in-Publication Data

Names: Hudak, Heather C., 1975- author.
Title: Pathways through South America / Heather C. Hudak.
Description: New York : Crabtree Publishing Company, [2020] |
  Series: The human path across the continents | Includes index.
Identifiers: LCCN 2019023330 (print) | LCCN 2019023331 (ebook) |
  ISBN 9780778766438 (hardcover) |
  ISBN 9780778766506 (paperback) |
  ISBN 9781427124029 (ebook)
Subjects: LCSH: Human ecology--South America--Juvenile literature. |
  Nature--Effect of human beings on--South America--Juvenile literature. |
  Physical geography--South America--Juvenile literature. | South America-
  -Environmental conditions--Juvenile literature.
Classification: LCC GF531 .H84 2020 (print) | LCC GF531 (ebook) |
  DDC 304.2098--dc23
LC record available at https://lccn.loc.gov/2019023330
LC ebook record available at https://lccn.loc.gov/2019023331

Crabtree Publishing Company

www.crabtreebooks.com   1-800-387-7650

Printed in the U.S.A./082019/CG20190712

Published in Canada
Crabtree Publishing
616 Welland Ave.
St. Catharines, Ontario
L2M 5V6

Published in the United States
Crabtree Publishing
PMB 59051
350 Fifth Avenue, 59th Floor
New York, New York 10118

Published in the United Kingdom
Crabtree Publishing
Maritime House
Basin Road North, Hove
BN41 1WR

Published in Australia
Crabtree Publishing
Unit 3–5 Currumbin Court
Capalaba
QLD 4157

CONTENTS

SOUTH AMERICA

The Human Path Across SOUTH AMERICA

Welcome to South America, a continent made up of 12 countries and one **territory**. From tropical rain forests and sandy deserts to **active volcanoes**, slow-moving glaciers, and lush **river basins**, South America has many contrasting landscapes. The continent is home to more than 420 million people who have adapted to live in almost every type of environment.

VENEZUELA

SURINAME
FRENCH GUIANA
(FRANCE)

COLOMBIA

GUYANA

ECUADOR

PERU

BRAZIL

BOLIVIA

CHILE

PARAGUAY

URUGUAY

ARGENTINA

ᴧᴧᴧ The Andes Mountains

⌐ ¬ The Amazon basin
⌐ ⌐

A canoe on the Amazon River

◄ **THE FIRST SOUTH AMERICANS** arrived on the continent about 11,000 years ago. At first, they settled along the Pacific coast and the Amazon River. These areas had plenty of freshwater to drink and fish to eat. Reed boats and canoes were used for fishing and to travel on lakes and rivers. Today, people use all types of transportation in South America, from buses to **cable cars**. No matter how people get from one place to another, a journey is a great way to explore a continent, as we will discover in this book.

Ruins of an Inca town in Peru

MASSIVE EMPIRES were built by ancient peoples in South America, including the Inca, Maya, and Aztecs. The Inca Empire was founded in the 1400s in the Andes Mountains of Peru. Over the next 100 years, it grew from what is now the northern border of Ecuador to central Chile. The Inca built a vast network of roads to connect each village and town in the empire. As a result, they were able to control much of the land.

By the 1500s, European settlers began to arrive, mainly from Spain and Portugal. Settlers took land from the **Indigenous** peoples. Many of them were killed in the fighting. Others were forced to work for their new rulers. Millions died of European diseases. European **colonists** also brought enslaved people from Africa to work on their farms. Today, traditional African, European, and Indigenous cultures all continue to influence life in South America.

RIO DE JANEIRO in Brazil is one of the many growing cities of South America today. From the mid-1900s, large numbers of people began to move to **urban** areas to work in **industries.** Today, about three-quarters of South Americans live in cities. These are vibrant places, with beautiful buildings and big businesses. However, in some areas, **poverty** and crime rates are high. Many cities are crowded, with huge populations. Basic services, such as electricity, waste disposal, and water, do not always work well there. Traffic pollution can also be a problem.

Looking down on Rio de Janeiro

Drive
THE PAN-AMERICAN HIGHWAY

PANAMA

Turbo

COLOMBIA

ECUADOR

Quito

— Pan-American Highway

Piura

BRAZIL

Lima   PERU

BOLIVIA

Tacna

Rio de Janeiro

CHILE

ARGENTINA

Buenos Aires

URUGUAY

Santiago   Montevideo

Quellón

Comodoro Rivadavia

Ushuaia

The Pan-American Highway (PAH) stretches across the Americas, from Prudhoe Bay, Alaska, to Ushuaia, Argentina. It is a system of roads that runs through 14 countries. Each country is responsible for building and caring for its own section of the PAH. The entire system is about 30,000 miles (48,000 km) in distance, making it the world's longest road. There is only one small break in the highway, through the swampy rain forest between Panama and Colombia.

⬇ **THE PAN-AMERICAN HIGHWAY** in South America starts in Turbo, Colombia. From there, it passes south through **humid** rain forests. The highway visits the major cities along the western coast, such as Quito, in Ecuador, and Lima, in Peru, before crossing into Chile. There, it passes through the Atacama Desert, the driest desert in the world. The route continues over the high Andes Mountains into Argentina. After thousands of miles, the highway ends in the snow and ice of Ushuaia, the southernmost town in the world.

Village on the PAH in Peru

A truck on the PAH in the Atacama Desert

⬇ **BUILDING THE PAH** has come at a price to the environment. Rain forests have been cut down to make room for the road, and farmlands have been destroyed. New towns and factories are often built near the highway, which causes more damage to the land. Many local people rely on farming to live. They often protest against new highway construction. They worry about losing their land and their way of earning a living to industry and urbanization.

Roadbuilding in the rain forest, Brazil

⬆ **CARGO CAN BE MOVED** quickly along the PAH. This helps grow South America's **economy.** It opens up opportunities for **trade** between communities and countries. It makes it easier to transport goods to cities along the coast, where they can be shipped to other continents. The highway also provides links to **remote** places, such as jungles and mountains that are hard to reach. But the drive is often risky. Sheer cliff drops, poor lighting, extreme temperatures, landslides, sand dunes, and wildlife are just a few hazards along the highway. Some parts of the highway are even washed out during the wet season.

PEOPLE
ALONG
THE WAY

Carlos is a farmer living in southern Colombia. Together with thousands of other Indigenous people, he took part in a protest on the Pan-American Highway. They demanded that the government uphold agreements that would improve their living conditions. They also protested against the loss of their traditional land to oil and mining companies. Their protest blocked traffic on the PAH for several days.

Take a Chiva Bus in COLOMBIA

Chivas are colorful wooden buses. They have an open-air frame with no windows or doors and long benches for seats. They were once the main way to travel on the bumpy dirt roads through the mountains in Colombia's countryside. Today, chivas are still used for transportation in **rural** areas. They are built to handle the rugged **terrain**. A common route travels between the towns of Jardín and Riosucio in the lush, green Andes Mountains.

COLOMBIA is located in the northwestern part of the continent. South America connects with Central America there. Colombia has snow-capped mountains, active volcanoes, large lakes, vast **savannas**, ocean coastlines, and rich rain forests. 49 million people live in Colombia. More than three-quarters of the population live in large cities. Bogotá and Medellin are the two biggest cities. About one-fifth of the population live near the Caribbean Sea. Colombia's three main **ports**, Barranquilla, Cartagena, and Santa Marta, are found there.

Map labels: CENTRAL AMERICA · Caribbean Sea · Barranquilla · Santa Marta · Cartagena · VENEZUELA · Medellin · Bogotá · Pacific Ocean · COLOMBIA · ECUADOR · BRAZIL · PERU

Inset map labels: Jardín · Route 25 · Route 25 · Route 25 · Riosucio · Road · Bus journey

Lake near Medellin

MOUNTAIN LANDSCAPES mean there is no easy way to travel from one part of Colombia to another. For a long time, large rivers were the main mode of travel across the country. Today, people use roads, but many are not paved. Rural mountain roads can be very narrow. The ride can be dangerous. Chivas are often used for travel in these places. The word chiva means "goat" in Spanish. Just like mountain goats, the buses are built to handle cliff ledges and rocky ground.

An unpaved mountain road

A chiva bus in Hispania, Colombia

CHIVA is also a slang word for "news." Travelers on the buses pass on news from one place to another. Chivas transport people, cargo, and animals as well. Anything that cannot fit inside is put on the roof. The buses are especially common in farming communities. They are an important connection between small towns and villages that do not have proper roads.

In big cities, such as Cartagena and Medellin, chivas are now also used for tour groups and events. They take tourists to popular attractions, such as museums and restaurants. Some chivas even have live bands and dancing on board. They contribute to Colombia's growing tourism industry.

Pause for REFLECTION

- Why is it difficult to travel through rural parts of Colombia?
- How have people adapted to be able to travel in their environments?
- How are chivas important to people in Colombia?

The Volcano Train in ECUADOR

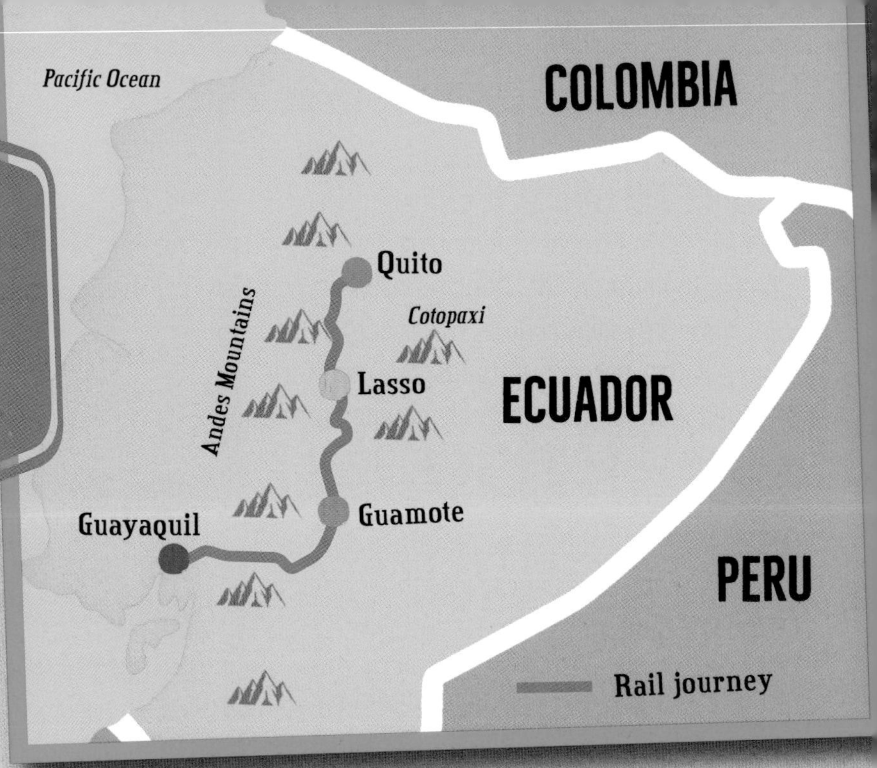

Ecuador is land of historical and natural wonders. It has so many different plant and animal species that it is one of only **17 megadiverse** countries in the world. There are many **colonial towns**, Inca ruins, and five **World Heritage Sites**. A great way to explore Ecuador is by riding the Tren Crucero train from the Pacific coast into the Andes Mountains. This is one of the world's most spectacular train rides.

Map labels: Pacific Ocean · COLOMBIA · Quito · Cotopaxi · Andes Mountains · Lasso · ECUADOR · Guayaquil · Guamote · PERU · Rail journey

▼ **GUAYAQUIL,** a port city on the Pacific coast, is the start of our journey. With a population of about 2.5 million, Guayaquil is the largest city in Ecuador. All kinds of products are manufactured there. There are also many shrimp farms. Nearly all goods shipped to Ecuador from other countries pass through Guayaquil. About half of the country's **exports** are sent through the port as well. They include bananas, coffee, and cacao.

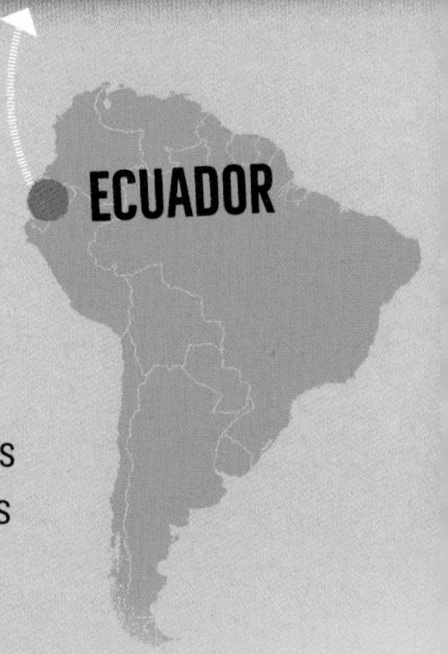

ECUADOR

The port at Guayaquil

Tren Crucero

▶ **TREN CRUCERO** has been called the world's most challenging railroad. Before the railway was built in 1908, there was no easy way to travel to and from Quito, Ecuador's capital, which sits high in the mountains. Horses and mules were used on trails. Building the railroad was difficult. Floods, landslides, and earthquakes often destroyed parts of the line.

Tren Crucero travels past more than 10 volcanoes and through thick rain forests as it climbs into the Andes. Along the way, it stops at Indigenous communities such as Guamote. It also passes Cotopaxi, one of the world's highest active volcanoes at 19,347 feet (5,897 m). Tren Crucero supports local communities through tourism. Tourists visit museums, stay in hotels, eat at restaurants, and buy souvenirs. This helps create jobs and bring **income** into Ecuador.

Quito with a view of the Cotopaxi volcano

Pause for REFLECTION

- How did the railway help connect people across Ecuador?
- Why was it so hard to build a railway into the mountains?
- How does the railway help the economy of Ecuador?

◀ **QUITO,** our final stop after 280 miles (450 km), is the oldest capital city in South America. Stretching along the slopes of two active volcanoes, it is also one of the highest capitals in the world. The city was built on the ruins of an Inca city from the 1500s. It is known for its Old Town, which looks the same today as it did when it was first built by the Spanish settlers. Today, Quito is home to about 2 million people. It is a major industrial center, known for making fabrics, medicines, leather objects, and more.

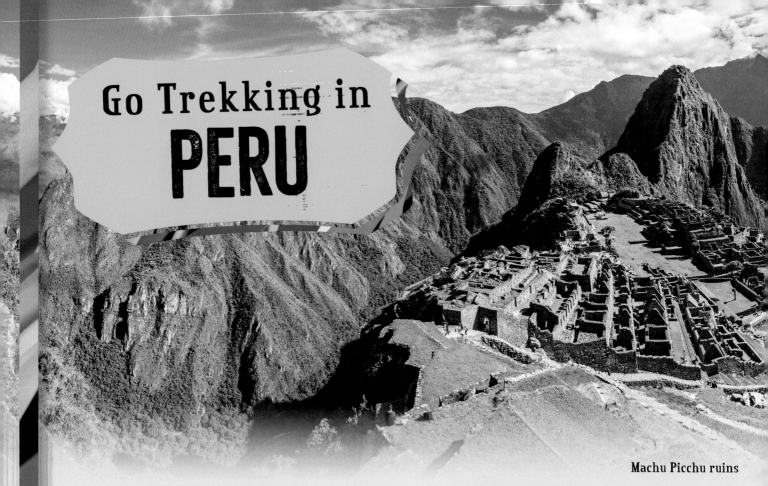

Go Trekking in PERU

Machu Picchu ruins

Between 1400 and 1533, the Inca Empire thrived in the Andes Mountains of Peru. The Incas called their empire Tahuantinsuyo, which meant "Land of the Four Corners." It was divided into four parts that met in its capital city of Cusco. Today, Cusco is the starting point for people who want to travel along the Inca Trail to Machu Picchu, an Inca city built high in the Andes Mountains.

⬆ **MACHU PICCHU** is one of the most popular tourist sites in Peru and the best-known remaining Inca site. It sits between two Andes peaks above the Urubamba River valley. The site has about 200 buildings made from blocks of stone. No one knows for sure what Machu Picchu was used for. Some **archaeologists** think it may have been a holiday home for the royal family.

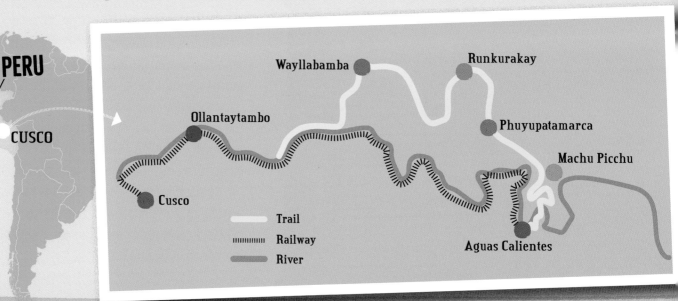

PERU

CUSCO

Wayllabamba

Runkurakay

Ollantaytambo

Phuyupatamarca

Machu Picchu

Cusco

Aguas Calientes

Trail
Railway
River

Palla runs a small bed and breakfast in Cusco that caters to tourists who come to walk the Inca Trail. She still shops at the local market for the food she prepares for her guests. She prefers it to the new supermarkets that have been built in town. She knows she is buying food grown in the mountains nearby, and wants to support the local farmers.

CUSCO, which originally grew up as a center for the local **agricultural** trade, has grown far bigger as a result of tourism. Machu Picchu brings a large amount of money into the local economy. About 1.4 million people visited in 2016.

But tourists have put the environment at risk. The garbage they produce piles up, while new construction and the number of visitors have damaged many ancient sites. For a long time, there were no limits to how the land near Machu Picchu was used. Today, the government of Peru has strict rules in place. For example, just 500 people can hike the Inca Trail each day.

Hikers on the Inca Trail

WALKING ALONG THE INCA TRAIL

to Machu Picchu brings many people to the region, although it is also possible by train and bus. The walk takes about four days. The mountainous route is challenging. It follows old paths that connect the local farming communities, such as the villages of Ollantaytambo and Wayllabamba. There are other Inca sites along the way too, including Runkurakay and Phuyupatamarca.

Street market, Cusco

Through CHILE BY RAIL

Railroad
Atacama Desert

PERU
BOLIVIA
CHILE
ARGENTINA

BOLIVIA
Mejillones
CHILE
Antofagasta
ARGENTINA

ARGENTINA

Valparaíso
Santiago
Rancagua
San Antonio

Mining is one of the biggest industries in Chile. The country produces large amounts of iron, nitrates, silver, and gold. It is also the world's largest copper producer. Several of the world's largest copper mines are found in Chile, and more than 50 percent of the country's exports are copper-related products. Trains are used to carry copper from mines to Chile's main ports on the Pacific Ocean. From there, copper is sent to countries such as Japan and China.

⬇ **THE ATACAMA DESERT** is where most of Chile's copper mines are found. A rail network transports copper from the desert to ports in Antofagasta and Mejillones. From there, it can be shipped across the continent and around the world. The railroad also links to the rest of Chile, as well as to Bolivia and Argentina. It is one of the busiest and most efficient rail lines in South America, and it earns a lot of money.

While mining has brought more people and money to the area, it has also created some problems. Mines need water to operate, but the Atacama Desert is one of the driest places in the world. The mines compete with local communities for what little water is available. They also pollute supplies of drinking water and cause air pollution.

A train in the Atacama Desert

Santiago's skyline

El Teniente copper mine

⬆ **SANTIAGO** is one of the most important financial centers in South America. Partly because of its links to the mining industry, the city now has many banks and insurance companies. The manufacturing industry has developed in Santiago as well. Food, fabric, shoes, and clothes are just some of the items made in Santiago. Railroads and highways connect the city to Chile's major ports, such as San Antonio and Valparaíso.

⬆ **MINING** helped make Chile one of the richest countries in South America. Over the centuries, many skilled workers have been drawn by this industry to settle in the country. Mining contributed to the development of Santiago, the capital of Chile. The world's largest underground copper mine, El Teniente, is only 60 miles (97 km) outside of the city. Copper from this mine is loaded onto trains, and brought to **processing plants** in Rancagua. From there, it is sent to the port of San Antonio for export.

Pause for
REFLECTION

- What would happen to Chile's economy if mining stopped in the Atacama Desert?
- How does mining benefit the people of Chile?
- How does it have a negative impact on them?

Bus Ride in ARGENTINA

Argentina is one of the most urbanized countries in the world. More than 90 percent of the country's 44 million people live in cities and towns. About one-third live in Buenos Aires, the capital city, and its surrounding areas. Millions of people **commute** through the sprawling city each day. Traffic jams can be a huge problem there. To help keep people moving, the city has spent a lot of money to upgrade its public transportation system.

ARGENTINA

BUENOS AIRES

BUS ROUTES
- Metrobus Cabildo
- Metrobus San Martin
- Metrobus Juan B. Justo
- Metrobus Au. 25 de Mayo
- Metrobus Sur
- Metrobus 9 de Julio
- Metrobus Paseo Colón

◄ **BUENOS AIRES** is a lively cultural center famous for tango dancing. It is also the economic hub of Argentina. Meat, paper, chemicals, and clothing are some of the items produced in the city. It is the main port in Argentina. Farmers send their crops to Buenos Aires by truck or train. From there, they are shipped across the continent and to other parts of the world.

Tango dancers in Buenos Aires

Traffic-free street, Buenos Aires

Pause for
REFLECTION

- Why is Buenos Aires so important to Argentina's economy?
- How does traffic impact daily life in Buenos Aires?
- What steps have been taken to solve traffic-related problems?

↑ **TRAFFIC JAMS** in Buenos Aires are some of the worst in the world. People spend hours traveling to and from work each day. To make matters worse, many drivers often run red lights, cut into traffic, and do not stop to let people cross the street. The high number of vehicles also pollutes the air. To help solve these problems, traffic is no longer allowed on some city streets. People can safely walk from one place to the next. There are also 119 miles (192 km) of bike lanes and 200 bike rental stations across the city.

↓ **THE BUS SYSTEM** has been improved to reduce traffic and get people around the city more easily. Special bus lanes have been added to keep buses moving when traffic comes to a halt. For instance, 9 de Julio Avenue is one of the widest and busiest streets in the world. The city made four of the 20 lanes for use by buses only. This system has made the trip faster for millions of people who commute each day. It has helped cut down the number of cars in the city center by 85 percent, and made it possible to travel in the city more quickly. Pollution is also lower since there are fewer cars on the road.

Bus lanes, 9 de Julio Avenue

Ferry Boat to URUGUAY

BRAZIL

Uruguay River

Negro River

URUGUAY

Paraná River

Colonia

Montevideo

Buenos Aires

Salado River

Río de la Plata

ARGENTINA

URUGUAY

Between Argentina and Uruguay, the Uruguay and Paraná Rivers meet to form the Río de la Plata **estuary**. The shores of the Río de la Plata are some of the most populated parts of Argentina and Uruguay. They are home to both Buenos Aires and Montevideo, the capital of Uruguay. Thousands of people travel between the two cities each day. The fastest way to get from one city to the other is by ferry boat.

A ferry on the Río de la Plata

BUQUEBUS

◄ **BUQUEBUS** is the most popular ferry service. The fast boats sail twice daily between the two capital cities. They can carry up to 1,000 people and 200 vehicles at a time. The trip takes just over two hours, sailing at up to 60 miles per hour (97 kph). Both business travelers and tourists use the ferries.

URUGUAY is one of the smallest countries in South America in size and population. Only about 3.5 million people live there. Most people earn a high income, and there is very little poverty. The government can afford to provide good services, such as housing, schools, and public transportation.

About two-thirds of Uruguay's people live along the coast of the Río de la Plata. Nearly 1.5 million people live in Montevideo, making it Uruguay's largest city. It is also Uruguay's main port. Large ocean vessels, cruise ships, and ferries stop there. The port is a main export site for beef, wool, and other goods. Montevideo's Old Town and central plaza are a short walk from the port. There are covered food markets, shops, and restaurants. Tourism is an important industry in Montevideo.

Covered market, Old Town, Montevideo

HUMAN ACTIVITIES are taking a toll on the Río de la Plata. The coastline has started to **erode**, and beaches are getting smaller. This is due to construction along the coast, and farming, forestry, and mining. For example, cutting down too many trees causes land to wear away. Ships also pollute the water, harming marine ecosystems. The government is working to protect the coast. For example, it is limiting waste disposal in the water.

Development on a Río de la Plata beach

Pause for REFLECTION

- Why do you think so many people live in the Río de la Plata region?
- What impact do human activities have on the environment around the Río de la Plata?

Cable Car in BOLIVIA

Set high in the Andes Mountains, the city of La Paz, Bolivia, reaches well into the clouds. At more than 11,900 feet (3,627 m) above sea level, it is the highest capital city in the world. The heart of the city lies in a deep **canyon** formed by the Choqueyapu River. From there, it rises up the canyon walls to the Altiplano **plateau** in the **highlands**. Each day, thousands of people travel between the highlands and the city center for work. The fastest way to make the trip is by cable car.

◀ **TRAFFIC** in the center of La Paz is a big problem. The narrow streets are too small for the number of vehicles that use them. It can take hours to travel just a few miles. Vehicles pollute the air and are very noisy. To help unclog traffic and reduce pollution, the government built a subway system in the sky.

A traffic jam in La Paz

Cable cars above La Paz

PEOPLE ALONG THE WAY

↑ MI TELÉFERICO is the world's longest urban cable car network. It cuts travel times and is a popular way for both tourists and locals to get around. Hundreds of thousands of people ride Mi Teléferico each day. The most popular journey is between central La Paz and the nearby city of El Alto, in the highlands. The ride offers stunning views of the mountains and the city below.

The people of La Paz and El Alto have welcomed the new cable car system. Elisa Marconi, a school teacher who lives in El Alto, has seen her journey to the shops in La Paz cut from two hours to 20 minutes. She also finds it easier to visit friends and family in La Paz, and she no longer worries about getting home quickly in an emergency.

Houses in El Alto

◀ EL ALTO is the second-largest city in Bolivia after Santa Cruz. Nearly 1 million people live there, compared to about 800,000 in La Paz. The new city grew quickly in the late 1900s, when land in La Paz began to cost too much for many people to buy. They started to move up the canyon walls outside the city, building their own brick and **adobe** houses. The air gets thinner at higher altitudes, making it harder to breathe, and there are strong winds. People in El Alto are generally poorer than people living lower down in La Paz. The new cable cars have been welcomed as a way of bringing the two communities together.

Cargo Boat Along the AMAZON

COLOMBIA
VENEZUELA **GUYANA**
SURINAME ┌ **FRENCH GUIANA (FRANCE)**

ECUADOR
Iquitos
Manaus
Amazon River
Santarém
Belém

Pucallpa

AMAZON RIVER BASIN

PERU

BRAZIL

BOLIVIA

PARAGUAY

■ Amazon River basin

The Amazon rain forest is the largest rain forest on Earth. Travel there can be hard. Thick jungle covers much of the land, and roads are often washed away by rain. That means that in parts of the rain forest, the Amazon River is the main mode of transportation. It is the widest and deepest river in the world. It is also the second-longest, after the Nile River in Africa.

About 30 million people live in the Amazon River basin. Most are found in cities along the river, such as Belém, Manaus, and Santarém in Brazil, and Iquitos and Pucallpa in Peru. There are roads to link these urban centers. But elsewhere around the Amazon, the river is the best way to travel.

⬇ **CARGO BOATS** are one of the ways people and goods are transported across the Amazon rain forest. The trip from the east of Brazil to the west of Peru can take up to three weeks. Conditions on the boats are harsh. There is often only one toilet for hundreds of people to share and no showers. The boats stop in many rural villages along the way to pick up and drop off people and cargo. There are no schedules. Locals often come on board to sell food while the boats are docked.

Amazon cargo boat, Peru

Logging in the Amazon rain forest

◀ **DEFORESTATION** and other human activities have caused a lot of damage to the Amazon basin. The rain forest's trees provide about one-fifth of the world's oxygen supply. Large areas of the rain forest are being cut down for agriculture. Many plant and animal species are endangered or at risk due to the loss of their habitat. The rain forest is also home to nearly 3 million Indigenous people who live off the land in remote areas. Deforestation threatens their traditional ways of life, which depend on the forest.

▼ **THE AMAZON BASIN** covers nearly 40 percent of South America, including much of Brazil. It stretches into parts of Peru, Ecuador, Bolivia, Colombia, Venezuela, Guyana, and Suriname. It is important to the economy of South America. Mahogany, cedar, and rosewood trees are cut down for **timber**. People harvest Brazil nut and rubber trees. Some land is used as pasture for cattle or to grow crops such as coffee, soybeans, and sugarcane. Large amounts of oil, iron ore, and bauxite are found in the basin. All these goods are exported to other countries around the world. Many people rely on the Amazon River for freshwater. The river is also used as a source of **hydroelectricity**.

The Amazon basin from the air

PEOPLE

ALONG THE WAY

Locals use Amazon cargo boats to visit families in other villages or to pick up supplies in cities and towns. Azucena, a Peruvian mother of two, has become used to the long boat rides. She sees the cargo boats as second homes. She is often on the boat for days at a time with her children, waiting for it to be full enough to leave. It is the only way she can get from her small Amazon village to bigger cities.

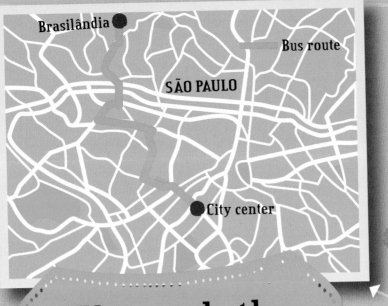

Brasilândia

Bus route

SÃO PAULO

City center

With a population of more than 21 million people, São Paulo is the largest city in South America. It is also one of the fastest-growing cities in the world. The city is made up of a core center and many suburbs, districts, and towns that have merged over time.

BRAZIL

Through the Streets of SÃO PAULO, BRAZIL

↓ **SÃO PAULO** is one of the richest cities in South America. Goods from furniture and food to medicines and cars are made in São Paulo. More than 10 percent of the population work in thousands of manufacturing plants. People also work in banks, retail stores, and transportation. But there are not enough jobs for everyone. Many people cannot find work. There is also a great deal of crime across the city.

Central São Paulo skyline

A city center park, São Paulo

LIKE MANY CITIES in South America, there is a big difference in the way people live in one part of the city to another. At the heart of São Paulo there are upscale and middle-class communities. Skyscrapers, movie theaters, high-end shops, museums, and parks line the streets. But many people who move to São Paulo to look for work cannot afford to live in the center. Instead, they live in poverty in **favelas** and slums, away from the center. They do not have access to proper housing, education, and health care. Many of these communities are in high-risk zones for floods and landslides too.

THE CITY CENTER is home to 12 million people. But nearly 10 million more live in poor communities on the edges of the city. Most work in the city center where there are more jobs and the pay is better. Often, there are no bus or train routes nearby. Many people have long walks to reach public transportation. When they arrive, they face long wait times. They spend hours traveling to and from work each day.

Houses in Brasilândia

BRASILÂNDIA, a favela on the edge of the city, is home to 300,000 people. It has no train, and a journey into the city center by bus can take nearly three hours. Most taxi companies will not go into the area due to crime and violence. A small company called Ubra hires local drivers to take people into areas that are not currently serviced by public transportation routes. Many drivers are glad to find work close to home and their families. It also lets them save money on gas and avoid heavy traffic in the city.

Pause for
REFLECTION

- Why are so many people moving to live in São Paolo?
- How does life differ for people in the city center and in communities on the edge of the city?

Water Taxi in SURINAME

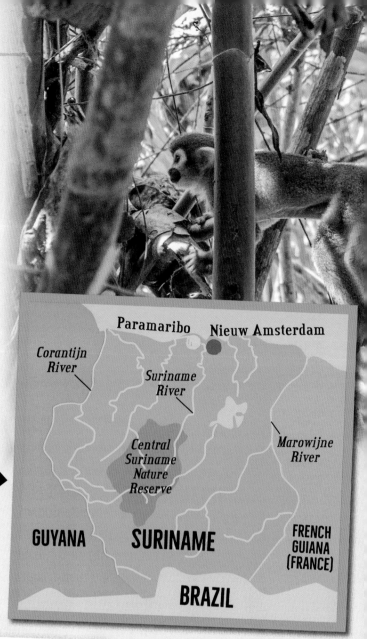

From thick forests to rushing rivers and exotic animals, Suriname is known for its natural beauty. Beyond Suriname's coastal area, which has some roads and public transportation systems, rivers and canals are used to get around. There are about 1,864 miles (3,000 km) of rivers across the country. The mighty Suriname, Corantijn, and Marowijne Rivers stretch from the Amazon basin to the Atlantic coast. Smaller rivers and **tributaries** form a water highway network that connects more remote regions.

SURINAME

Paramaribo Nieuw Amsterdam

Corantijn River

Suriname River

Central Suriname Nature Reserve

Marowijne River

GUYANA **SURINAME** FRENCH GUIANA (FRANCE)

BRAZIL

Dutch-style houses, Paramaribo

◀ **SURINAME** is one of the smallest countries in South America. Less than 600,000 people live there. But it is one of the most diverse countries on the continent. Most people are the descendants of laborers from India and the island of Java, or enslaved people from Africa who were brought there by the Dutch colonists. Their culture and heritage remains strong to this day. It can be seen in the range of traditional foods, music, languages, and art across the country. Most people live in urban areas along the coast, including the capital, Paramaribo.

Stanley owns a water taxi that he keeps at Domburg, 6 miles (10 km) up the river from Paramaribo. He takes locals to and from the main town, agreeing on a fee based on how many people are traveling and what they are transporting. He also makes extra money from the international sailors who bring their yachts into Domburg's marinas.

Squirrel monkeys, Suriname rain forest

⬆ **THE AMAZON RAIN FOREST** plays an important role in the country's economy. It covers about 95 percent of the land. Instead of cutting down the trees to sell as timber, Suriname plans to preserve its forests. It hopes to make **ecotourism** a key source of income. There are 11 national **nature reserves** across the country. The Central Suriname Nature Reserve is one of the largest protected rainforest areas on Earth. For now, mining is the top industry in Suriname. **Minerals**, such as gold, are especially rich in the coastal plain. But these resources are running out.

⬇ **WATER TAXIS** are a common way for tourists and locals to get around outside Paramaribo. Taxis sail down the many rivers through the vast rain forest. They stop at towns and villages, and **plantations** where coffee and cocoa are grown. Some old plantation houses have been turned into hotels for tourists. Water taxis also take visitors to Fort Nieuw Amsterdam. It was built by the Dutch in the mid-1700s to protect the crops along the river from enemy attack. Today, the fort is a museum.

A Suriname water taxi

CENTRAL AMERICA

Maracaibo   Amuay   Caracas

Puerto Cabello   Puerto La Cruz

GUYANA

VENEZUELA

Cargo Truck in VENEZUELA

COLOMBIA

● Oil fields
— Oil pipelines

Oil refinery, Venezuela

Venezuela is a country in crisis. People struggle to pay for food and basic services there. Wages are low, and there is not enough food to eat. Many communities face cuts to electricity. Public transportation has come to a halt in most parts of the country. It costs too much to pay for the parts and fuel that buses and cars need to run. Many people now rely on cargo trucks to get from one place to another.

⬆ **VENEZUELA** has some of the largest oil reserves on Earth. When the price of oil was high, this made it a wealthy nation. Most of Venezuela's income comes from the oil it sells to other parts of the world. It uses the money from oil sales to **import** many goods from other countries, including food and medicine. The money also pays for services such as schools, roads, water, and sewer systems.

Empty store shelves, Santa Elena de Uairén, Venezuela

Carmen Hernández is a housemaid in Maracaibo, Venezuela's second-largest city. She relies on crowded, run-down cargo trucks to get to work because a bus may never come. Carmen cannot afford to lose her job and sometimes ends up walking for dozens of blocks if a truck doesn't come. Life has become so hard that she is thinking about leaving Venezuela to live in another country.

⬆ FALLING OIL PRICES mean Venezuela does not have the money to import many products. Stores have been left with empty shelves. The government does not have the funds to keep up basic services. Hospitals are run-down and people cannot get the care they need. As a result, many people have fled Venezuela to other countries in South America as **refugees**. More than 4 million people have left.

Transportation is another big problem in Venezuela. People who can afford cars have a hard time keeping them running. The number of buses across the country has been reduced from 280,000 to 30,000. The lack of transportation has had a huge impact. Many people now look for work closer to home so they do not have to travel too far. Others rely on cargo trucks to get around instead.

▶ CARGO TRUCKS are a main way people can still get around in Venezuela. But they are unsafe. People stand on the back and hold on to metal rails. Some have been hurt or have died falling off the trucks. Cargo trucks do not have regular routes, and they do not run on a schedule. It is common for people to walk many miles each day.

Cargo truck, Caracas

GLOSSARY

active volcano A volcano that has erupted at least once in the past 10,000 years

adobe Type of clay used for building and brickmaking

agricultural Relating to agriculture, or activities to do with growing crops and raising livestock

archaeologist A person who studies the people of the past through the traces they left behind

cable car A form of transportation where people are carried through the air in cabins, or cars, suspended from moving ropes of wire or cables

canyon A deep valley, through which a river usually flows, with steep cliffs on either side

colonial towns Towns founded by colonists when settling in another country

colonists People who settle and take control of a new land or region on behalf of a government

commute To travel regularly from where you live to where you work, which may be some distance away

economy The system by which goods and services are made, bought, sold, and used

ecotourism Vacation travel that aims not to leave a bad effect on the environment of the places visited. It often takes place in protected natural areas.

erode Gradually wear away due to natural forces such as wind and water

estuary A body of water found where freshwater and the sea meet

exports Goods sent to be sold in another country

favela A Brazilian word for a poor area of a city made up of self-built houses or shacks; a shantytown

highlands Areas of hilly, higher ground

humid Damp

hydroelectricity Electricity made by using the power of moving water

import To bring goods into a country to be sold

income The amount of money a person, group, or region makes

Indigenous Describes people who naturally exist or live in a place rather than arrived from elsewhere

industries Groups of companies that produce goods and services

megadiverse Having a very large variety of life, with many different plant and animal species

mineral A solid, nonliving substance found in nature, often taken out of the ground by mining

nature reserve An area of land managed in a way that protects its wildlife, plants, and landscape

plantations Large farms used to grow crops

plateau An area of mainly flat, high ground

ports Places where ships load and unload cargo

poverty The state of not having enough money for basic needs, such as food, clothing, and shelter

processing plant A factory where minerals taken from mines, such as copper, are turned into metal to be used in industries or in construction

refugees People who have been forced to leave their own country for reasons such as war or famine

remote Describes a place far from large settlements

river basin The area of land from which water drains into a particular river

rural Having to do with the country

savannas Grassy plains with few trees

terrain The ground, or a piece of land

territory A place owned or ruled by a government

timber Wood used for building

trade Buying and selling goods and services

tributaries Streams or rivers that flow into a larger river or lake

urban Having to do with cities or towns

World Heritage Sites Places that have special cultural, historical, or scientific importance

Further INFORMATION

BOOKS

DK. *Aztec, Inca, & Maya*. DK Eyewitness Books, 2011.

Hyde, Natalie. *Amazon Rainforest Research Journal*. Crabtree Publishing, 2018.

Rockett, Paul. *Mapping South America*. Crabtree Publishing, 2017.

WEBSITES

www.worldwildlife.org/places/amazon
Learn all about the plants, animals, and people of the Amazon.

www.ducksters.com/geography/southamerica.php
Facts and figures about South America, with links to further information about its individual countries.

www.visitperu.com/visit-peruinfo/english/detalle-destinos.php?cod_destino=10
Find out more about the ancient Inca ruins of Machu Picchu.

INDEX

ABOUT THE AUTHOR

Heather C. Hudak has written hundreds of children's books. When she's not writing, Heather enjoys traveling the world, from the beaches of Brazil to the African savanna. She also loves camping in the mountains near her home with her husband and many rescue pets.